GoNoodle®

RAINY DAY PARTY!

The Ultimate
Rainy Day
Activity Book

ISBN 978-1-338-81391-3

10 9 8 7 6 5 4 3 2 1   22 23 24 25 26
Printed in the U.S.A.   40
First printing 2022

Book design by Two Red Shoes Design
Stock photos © Shutterstock.com.

Scholastic Inc.

IT'S RAINING!

Hey, friend! We're the GoNoodle Champs. Welcome to the Champiverse!

When it rains in the Champiverse, we throw an awesomely amazing RAINY DAY PARTY. And guess what? You're invited!

When the clouds gather outside, it's time to get excited for all the indoor fun that's about to go down. Join us for a bunch of boredom-busting, body-bopping activities and games. You'll make music, make treats, make moves—and you won't even have to leave the house.

IT'S POURING!

Some of the games, crafts, and recipes in this book use common household items. Make sure you ask an adult for permission and help before doing any of these activities. That way, you'll have the best, safest, most carefree experience.

Don't let the rain dampen your spirit. It's party time!

MEET THE CREW

Allow us to introduce ourselves. We're the hosts of this RAINY DAY PARTY, and we're thrilled to meet you. Take a moment to say hi, then color the pictures.

OM PETALHEAD

I'm cool, calm, and collected. Breathe with me.

NOVA STEAMSTEEN

I love science, tech, engineering, art, and math!

FLO YO

I love taking shellfies on my shell phone!

McPUFFERSON

I'm curious and I have limitless amounts of energy. Come on, time to get movin'!

SQUATCHY

There's nothing I love more than rock 'n' roll!

ZAPP VON DOUBLER

I'm a genius who loves to invent things!

FLASH BOLTON

I'm full of spark, and I love exploring. My next adventure can't come soon enough!

SUPER RUFUS

Traveling the world and playing soccer in every country is my GOOAALLL!

COACH TERRY

I'm Coach Terry, and I'm here to help you get in shape!

THE BEST TEES

We're all about positivity, kindness, and sweet dance moves!

MOOSE TUBE

Come chant and cheer along with us. Let's go!

4

FIND YOUR CALM

Rain Breathing

Let's make it rain! Don't worry—you won't get wet. You're just going to breathe like the wind and move like the rain. This will focus your mind and get your body ready for all the fun ahead.

1 Stand tall with your feet hip-width apart. Relax your shoulders and let your arms hang down by your sides.

2 Take a deep, slow breath in through your nose.

3 With your lips pursed, breathe out through your mouth. Make a big "whoosh" sound as the air comes out.

Hey, that breath sounded just like the wind. Nice! Now let's match your breathing with some moves. Keep going!

4 As you breathe in through your nose, gently lift your arms above your head. Fill your lungs with air as you reach your fingers toward the rain clouds in the sky.

5 Sweep your arms down in front of you as you breathe out of your mouth with a "whoosh" sound.

6 Try this a few more times. Raise your arms with each breath in. Bring your arms down like falling rain with each whooshing breath out.

LET'S MOVE!

Alive, Alert, Awake!

Now let's start to build some energy and positivity. Sing along and follow these simple moves to hype yourself up!

I'm alive . . .

1 Tap your hands on your head.

. . . alert . . .

2 Tap your hands on your shoulders.

. . . awake . . .

3 Softly bend to tap your hands on your knees.

. . . enthusiastic!

4 Bend over to touch your toes, then stand back up with your arms reaching high!

I'm alive, alert, awake, enthusiastic!

5 Repeat those moves! Tap your head, shoulders, knees, and toes.

I'm alive, alert, awake . . .

6 Tap your head, shoulders, and knees.

. . . I'm awake, alert, alive . . .

7 Reverse it! Tap your knees, shoulders, and head in that order.

. . . I'm alive, alert, awake, enthusiastic!

8 One more time! Tap your head, shoulders, knees, and toes. Throw your arms up!

Rainy Day Challenge

Can you speed it up? Pick up the pace each time. Don't forget to match the moves to the words. See how far you get before you're a blur of arms and noise!

HoW To!

Pump It Up!

Look at you! You're focused, you're awake, and you're ready for more. Keep that energy pumping with this warm-up routine.

Circle Your Arms

1 Reach your arms out to either side of your body. Keep them in line with your shoulders and parallel to the floor.

2 Keep your arms straight while you make five big circles going forward.

3 Now go the other way! Make five big circles going backward.

Cross Your Body

1 Stand with your feet wide apart. Reach your arms out on either side of your body.

2 Reach your left hand to your right foot. Try to keep your legs straight as you bend from the waist.

3 Come back up, then reach your right hand to your left foot.

4 Do five more cross-body toe touches. You've got this!

Lunge Side to Side

1 Stand with your feet hip-width apart. Step your left leg out to the side with your toes pointed forward.

2 Bend your left knee and keep your right leg straight.

3 Return to the center, then step your right leg out to the side. Bend your right knee while keeping your left leg straight.

4 Do five more lunges, going from side to side. Step, bend, repeat!

Using your whole body like this gets your muscles and joints all warmed up.

LET'S MOVE!

You Got This!

Do things seem a little gloomy when it's raining outside? It's okay to feel that way! See if you can perk things up with some motivational moves.

You got this! I got this!

1 Start skipping in place.

There's nothing new that we can't do. Woo!

2 Keep skipping, then jump into the air when you say "Woo!"

You got this! I got this!

3 Jump from side to side.

You and I . . .

4 Stand in place. Point your fingers out, then point them in toward yourself.

. . . are super fly.

The BEST TEES

We got this!

5 Pump your arms out to the side. Then bring them in and cross your arms over your chest.

WE GOT THIS

6 Jump up and down on the spot while pumping your arms in the air.

What is something you dream of doing? Think big! You can do anything!

MAKE IT!

Rain in a Jar

If you can't control the weather outside, control it in a jar! Ask an adult to help you make your very own swirling, whirling mini rainstorm.

What You Need

Water
Jar or glass
Shaving foam
  (not shaving gel)
Food coloring

What You Do

1. Add water to your jar or glass until it's about ¾ full.
2. Make a fluffy cloud by spraying shaving cream on top of the water. Don't make your cloud too thick!
3. Squeeze droplets of food coloring onto the cloud. Within a few minutes, "raindrops" will swirl into the water.

You can use any color for the rain. Try a mix of colors to see how it looks. Get creative!

FIND YOUR CALM

Swirling

Sometimes our thoughts and feelings can swirl around inside us—just like the rain in your jar! Try this breathing exercise to calm those thoughts and feelings.

1 Rest back in your chair or settle into a comfortable seat on the floor.

2 Think of your rain jar. The colors are swirling around in the water.

3 Just for now, imagine that those swirling colors are your thoughts and feelings.

4 Let's try to settle those swirling thoughts and emotions with long, slow breaths. First, place your hands on your belly.

5 Breathe in and make your exhale longer than usual. The swirling is starting to settle.

6 Keep breathing in and exhaling this way until the swirling has slowed down and maybe even stopped altogether!

You can do this anytime you're feeling mixed up inside or just want to feel calm and relaxed.

LET'S MOVE!

Fabio's Meatball Run

Fabio is delivering meatballs to his grandmoose. (That's Fabio's grandmother!) He must go quickly so the food doesn't get cold. Race with him and watch out for silly obstacles along the way!

1 Start by jogging in place. Oh no! A flock of birds is flying toward your head. DUCK!

2 That was close! Get back up and keep jogging in place. See that banana peel? Don't slip on it. JUMP!

3 Great jump! Keep on jogging. Is that a piano?! It's way too big to jump over. DODGE LEFT!

4 You've got quick reflexes! Don't stop jogging. A soccer ball is hurtling toward you. KICK IT!

5 You're almost there. Run, run, run! Watch out for the duck. It's riding a bear?! DODGE RIGHT!

DODGE RIGHT!

6 There's Grandmoose's house! Quickly, run! Don't step in the spaghetti. JUMP! You made it!

JUMP!

Rainy Day Challenge

Imagine you're out on a jog and each of these items gets in your way. What moves would you use to get past each one? Try it!

- A hole in the road
- A bunch of balloons
- A Frisbee flying toward you
- A cartwheeling cat
- A pizza falling from the sky

GAME TiME!

Puddle Crossing

Ask an adult for permission first. Then make an obstacle course in your very own home!

What You Do

1. Find the right place to set up your obstacle course. It should be a clear area without any sharp corners, heavy objects you could run into, or fragile things that could break.

2. Set up some obstacles any way you like. Stick with soft, safe things! Here are a few ideas:
   - Arrange pieces of construction paper on the floor.
   - Toss some pillows or cushions on the floor.
   - Roll up towels or blankets and place them among your other obstacles.

3. Time to play! Imagine the obstacles are puddles of rain. As you go through your obstacle course, avoid all the puddles. Good luck!

Rainy Day Challenge

Level up your game with a few simple mods.

- Arrange the puddles differently.
- Crawl through the course without standing.
- Hop through the course on one leg.
- Play with siblings or friends. Who can make it through in the fewest moves?

Pitter-Patter Percussion

Doesn't the rain sound awesome as it patters against the windows? Ask an adult for help. Then play along with the beat!

What You Need
Uncooked rice or dried beans
Clean, empty tin can
Scissors
Balloon
Rubber band
Chopsticks (optional)

What You Do
1. Put a handful of rice or beans into the empty can.
2. Cut off the end of the balloon. Stretch the balloon over the top of the can.
3. Stretch a rubber band around the top of the can to secure the balloon.
4. Make some rhythms by shaking your music-maker. You can even use chopsticks as drumsticks!

LET'S MOVE!

Peanut Butter in a Cup

Do you need a quick burst of energy? Get up and get moving with this bopping routine!

Peanut butter in a cup, we sing this song to pump us up.

1 Run in place and clap your hands.

Bang bang, choo-choo train! Come on you, do your thing!

2 Run in place and pump your arms in front of you.

Why not? Why not?

3 Stand still for a moment and shrug your shoulders.

From the left to the right, from the left to the right.

4 Wiggle your hips from left to right.

Moose Tube

Left, right, left, right, left, right, left, right, left, right!

5 Keep wiggling your hips faster and faster!

Peanut butter in a cup, we sing this song, now we're pumped up!

6 Run in place and clap your hands. Finish with a big jump!

Rainy Day Challenge
Crack up your friends with this silly joke!

Knock, knock!
Who's there?
Peanut.
Peanut who?
Peanut, butter open the door!

Make NB+J Tacos

You've pumped yourself up with peanut butter in a cup. Now have a snack break with nut butter in a taco!

What You Need
1 plastic cup
4 slices of bread
⅓ cup nut butter
⅓ cup jelly
½ cup chopped strawberries*
½ cup blueberries
¼ cup crushed graham crackers
4 teaspoons honey

STEP 1

Use the cup to cut the bread slices into circles.

*Ask an adult to help you cut the fruit.

Spread the nut butter on each circle of bread.

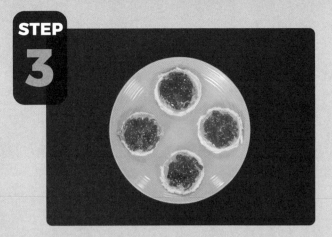

Spread the jelly on top of the nut butter.

STEP 4

Add a few strawberries and blueberries to each circle.

STEP 5

Sprinkle some crushed graham crackers on top of each circle. Drizzle each circle with some honey.

IT'S TACO TIME!

Fold the bread over and enjoy your NB+J taco fiesta!

Strike a Pose

Get the party pumping with this silly game. All you need is some music and one or more people to play with.

1 Assign one person to be the DJ. They get to choose a song to play.

2 Hit the music! When the DJ presses play, everybody dances.

3 When the DJ pauses the music, everybody freezes.

4 The DJ picks one of the Champs and yells out its name. Hold up the next page of the book so everyone can see the Champ.

5 Strike a pose! Each dancer copies the Champ's pose. Stay frozen like that until the music starts again.

6 The DJ can pause the music at random and pick as many Champs as they like until the song ends.

7 For the next song, make someone else the DJ.

McPUFFERSON

OM PETALHEAD

ZAPP VON DOUBLER

FLO YO

SQUATCHY

SUPER RUFUS

FIND YOUR CALM

Grow Gratitude

Are you buzzing with energy from all that dancing? Chill out and relax! This exercise will calm you down and lift your spirits.

1 Breathe in through your nose and out through your mouth.

2 With each breath, bring your attention to a different part of your body and relax it. Start with your face. Breathe in, then relax your face as you breathe out.

3 Notice your shoulders and arms as you breathe in. Relax them as you breathe out.

4 Notice your legs and feet as you breathe in. Relax them as you breathe out.

5 Now that your body is a little more relaxed, close your eyes. Breathe in and bring your attention to your heart.

6 Think about something or someone that you're grateful for. Keep taking deep breaths and think of all the reasons why you're grateful for this something or someone.

7 Feel this gratitude in your heart. Let this feeling spread to each part of your body as you breathe in and out. Fill your body with gratitude.

8 Remember this feeling and slowly open your eyes. Move forward with your day filled with gratitude and love.

LET'S MOVE!

Skip Count and Dance!

Need to pass the time while you wait for the rain to stop? Count away the hours with some numbers and dancing!

1 Skip count to 100 while you march in place. 2, 4, 6, 8, 10 . . . keep marching and counting!

2 Skip count to 100 while you do jumping jacks. 5, 10, 15, 20 . . . keep jumping and counting!

3 Skip count to 100 while you wave your arms around. 10, 20, 30 . . . keep waving and counting!

4 Skip count to 100 while you bend your knees. 20, 40, 60 . . . keep bending and counting!

100 BY 25'S!

5 Skip count to 100 while you nod your head. 25, 50 . . . keep nodding and counting!

Moose Tube

100

Rainy Day Challenge
Can you count to 200 by 2's, 5's, 10's, 20's, and 25's? Try it!

LET'S MOVE!

Work up a Storm!

It's raining outside, but you can work up a storm indoors! Get ready for the Ultimate Champ Training boot camp. Follow these moves from my playbook.

Crumb Bum

Champs clean up! Bend your knees and press your hips back to do a squat. Pretend you're picking up crumbs from the floor while you're bent down. Squat and stand, squat and stand. Keep squatting and standing, faster and faster, until you've picked up all the crumbs.

The Champoline

Jump on the Champoline! Bring your legs out wide for a straddle jump. Jump on one leg. Then jump on the other leg. Do some freestyle jumping. Go faster! Go higher! Go wild!

Kneat-o

Punch your arms down to help this Champ knead some dough. Get out the air bubbles. Go harder! Go faster! Then punch out in front of you like the dough is on the wall. Punch it! Knead it! Now punch up like the dough is on the ceiling.

Slo-mo

Change the pace! Run in place in slow motion. Now spread your legs out in a straddle jump. Raise one foot, then the other foot. Take it slooooowly. Finish up with some slow and steady squats.

That was awesome! Give yourself a self-five!

HOW! TO!

Make a Banana Crunch Pop

It's time for a healthy snack to keep you fueled for more movement and fun. Bring some color to a gray day with this treat!

What You Need
Baking sheet
Wax paper
1 cup strawberry yogurt
2 cups fruity cereal
2 bowls
8 wooden ice pop sticks
4 bananas, cut in half*
8 resealable sandwich bags

STEP 1

Line the baking sheet with wax paper. Put the yogurt and the cereal into two separate bowls.

*Ask an adult to help you cut the fruit.

2

Put a wooden ice pop stick into the cut side of each banana half.

3

Dip a banana in the yogurt and then roll it in the cereal until it's totally covered.

4

Put the banana on the baking sheet. Repeat with the remaining bananas. Then put the baking sheet in the freezer for 1 hour.

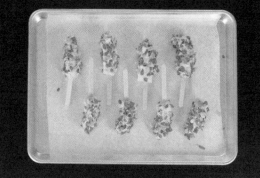

5

Take the baking sheet out of the freezer. Put each banana in a plastic bag and put them back in the freezer for 2 more hours.

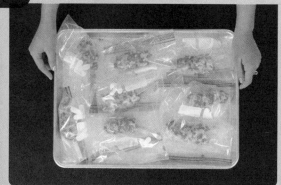

6

Enjoy!

LET'S MOVE!

D-I-S-C-O

What happens when you spell out the letters in the word *DISCO*? You get a rainy day dance break! Sing and dance along.

D-I-S-C-O. That's the way we disco.

1 Step from side to side. Roll your arms in front of you as you step.

Show us how you disco!

2 Point one arm up to the side. Then bring that arm down across your body and point it toward the ground. Keep pointing your arm up and down to the beat!

I slide to the side. Disco!

3 Sweep your arms up as you slide to the side.

Moose Tube

I roll my eyes.

4 Step back to the center. As you step, circle your hands on either side of your head.

I kick my feet.

5 Kick your leg and clap your hands underneath it. Kick your other leg and clap your hands underneath it.

Do the super freak!

6 Freestyle! Dance any way you like. Just keep moving and grooving!

Rainy Day Dance Party

Let's keep the party going with a rainy day game. Grab a pencil and a paper clip to get started. There's only one rule to this game: Just have fun!

1. Place the paper clip on the red dot in the center of the wheel.

2. Lightly press the nib of your pencil on the red dot. Hold the end of the pencil to keep it upright.

3. Using your other hand, spin the paper clip around the pencil nib.

4. Look at where the paper clip lands. What rainy day thing is shown?

5. Make up a dance inspired by this thing!

Rainy Day Challenge

Can you make up different dances based on different weather? How would you dance like a sunny day? How would you dance like falling snow? Use your imagination!

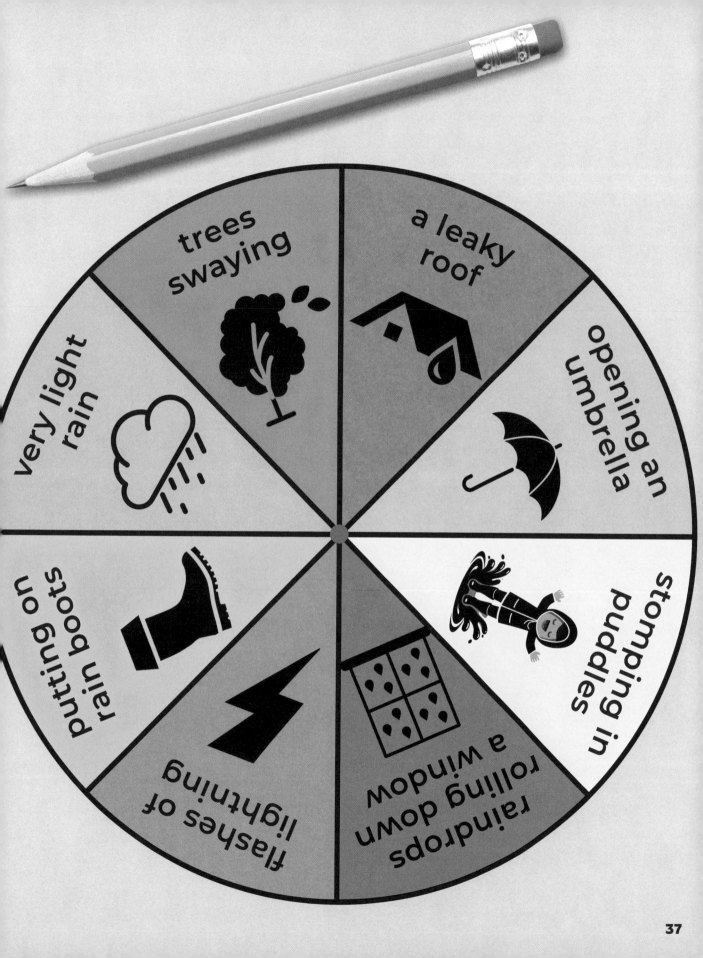

trees swaying

a leaky roof

opening an umbrella

very light rain

stomping in puddles

putting on rain boots

raindrops rolling down a window

flashes of lightning

LET'S MOVE!

Dance like This Dude

You've been coming up with some really creative dances! If you're running out of ideas, we've got you covered. Just dance like this dude!

Dance like this dude. Oh yeah!

1 Lift your elbows to shoulder height, letting your hands hang down. Bounce from side to side.

Dance like this dude. Punch it!

PUNCH IT!

2 Bounce up and down while you punch your arms in the air.

Dance like this dude. Monkey!

MONKEY!

3 Run in place with your legs straddled wide. Raise one arm above your head and point the other arm in front of you.

Dance like this dude. Snake!

SNAKE!

4 Wiggle your body like a snake. Hold your arms out to your sides and wiggle them, too!

Rainy Day Challenge

Now try to come up with your own dance moves! Can you dance like a giraffe? What would it look like to move like an elephant? Try to dance like a fish! Just have fun with it!

Dance like this dude. Pony!

PONY!

5 Put your hands on your hips and trot like a pony!

Dance like this dude. Yeah!

6 Now mix it up! Combine all the moves into one wild dance.

39

HOW TO! Make Shadow Puppets

Still raining outside? Good. Now you can make shadow puppets! All you need is a wall, a light, and your hands.

The Dog

Put your hands halfway between the light and the wall. Stretch your hand out so your four fingers are pointing forward. Bend your pointer finger and stick up your thumb to make the ear. See if you can move your fingers to make the dog's mouth open. Woof!

The Deer

Hold out one hand. Bring your pointer and pinky fingers over your middle and ring fingers. Fold down your thumb. This is the deer's face. Bend your other hand back at the wrist and curl your fingers to make the antlers. Rest the antlers on top of the deer's head.

The Grumpy Old Man

Turn your hand upside down and make a fist. Stick out your middle knuckle to make his nose. Use your thumb as his mouth.

The Bird

Put your hands halfway between the light and the wall. Link your thumbs together. Stretch out your hands to make the wings.

Rainy Day Challenge

Can you make a story using all these characters? Put on a puppet show using your new talent!

LET'S MOVE!

Animal Poses

The Deer

You made some pretty cool animals with your hands! Now do it with your whole body.

1 Bend both legs and touch your front foot to your back knee.

2 Lie forward like a sleeping deer. Hold this pose for five seconds.

The Dog

Get down on your hands and knees. Keep your hands on the floor while you straighten your legs. Turn your body into an upside-down V. Hold this pose for five seconds.

The Bird

1 Leave your front leg where it is and extend your back leg behind you.

2 Lean forward and back five times.

3 It's a pigeon!

Reach for the Rainbow

What comes after the rain? That's right. A rainbow! Jump up and try to touch that rainbow by doing a burpee. Here's how!

STEP 1
Put both of your hands on the ground. Kick out your legs behind you.

STEP 2
Jump your feet to your hands.

STEP 3
Spring up and lift your hands.

Rainy Day Challenge
How many burpees can you do in a row?

Melt into a Puddle

After all that jumping and moving, take a moment to cool off and wind down. Release all that energy with some rest and relaxation.

1 Stand up in a spot with a little space around you.

2 Cross your arms and hold your shoulders with your hands. Carefully tuck your chin down and in.

3 Tighten as many muscles in your body as you can. Keep frozen and still.

4 Little by little, begin to melt. Let your chin stay low as your face softens. Let your shoulders melt and release. Hands let go; arms glide down to your sides. Let your legs melt, too.

5 Soften and melt. Try to melt all the way to the floor. Let yourself be a puddle.

6 Breathe out. Feel at ease.

Goodbye!

Thanks for coming to our RAINY DAY PARTY. You brought so much energy and so much joy. You're a total champ!

You've reached the end of this book, but the party isn't over. These activities aren't just for a rainy day. You can do them anytime and anywhere! Share all the fun with your friends and family. Try all the challenges. Just keep moving.

Be creative, be silly, be your best self—no matter the weather.

You're amazing!

Bye!

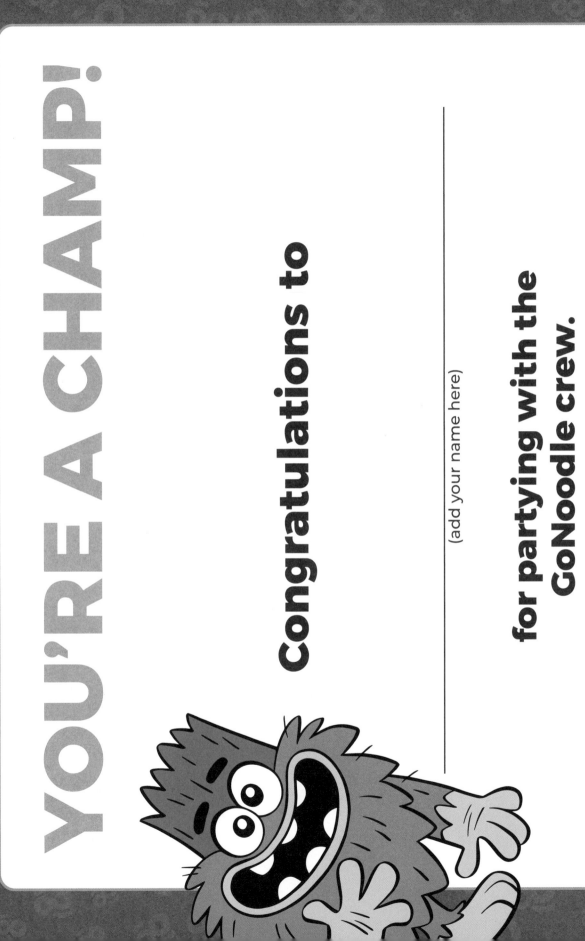

YOU'RE A CHAMP!

Congratulations to

_____

(add your name here)

for partying with the GoNoodle crew.

Can you find something white?

clock

Can you find something blue?

cup

Can you find something green?

chair

Can you find something more than 10 years old?

pillow

Can you find something less than 1 year old?

ball

shoe

box

toothbrush

toy

pencil

Can you find something soft?

key

Can you find something red?

bottle

Can you find something smooth?

book

hat

Can you find something with your name on it?

picture

bag

umbrella

Can you find something shiny?

spoon

Can you find something see-through?

sock

Can you find something pink?

button

Can you find something black?

zipper

Can you find something yellow?